A *Grief Unobserved*

Helping parents and carers with early childhood bereavement

Maggie Kindred

PNEUMA SPRINGS PUBLISHING UK

First Published in 2012 by:
Pneuma Springs Publishing

A Grief Unobserved
Copyright © 2012 Maggie Kindred

Maggie Kindred has asserted her right under the Copyright, Designs
and Patents Act, 1988, to be identified as Author of this Work

Pneuma Springs

British Library Cataloguing in Publication Data

Kindred, Maggie, 1940-
A grief unobserved : helping parents and carers with early
childhood bereavement.
1. Bereavement in children.
I. Title
155.9'37'083-dc23

ISBN-13: 9781907728372

Pneuma Springs Publishing
A Subsidiary of Pneuma Springs Ltd.
7 Groveherst Road, Dartford Kent, DA1 5JD.
E: admin@pneumasprings.co.uk
W: www.pneumasprings.co.uk

Dedication

To my partner Michael for his wonderful love and support in writing this book

To 'Taffy' who was such a gifted and caring therapist for Em

To Dorothy for filling in so many gaps in Em's early life

To Jennifer Fox for her honest critique of the manuscript

To all my colleagues and clients, with great affection and respect

To my friends for their unfailing support during difficult times

Introduction

There is a wonderful book by C S Lewis which describes the progress of the relationship between himself and a partner whom he meets late in life. They are each delighted to have found the other but very soon she develops cancer and dies. He describes the process of his grief in coming to terms with his loss: how it challenges his faith and shakes his stability to the core - the 'grief observed' which most adults will experience at some time in their lives.

This book is about the grief *not* observed, that of very young children. It has been written because the author's personal and professional experience leads her to believe that, despite the attention given to bereavement counselling in recent years, there is little to help children and their carers where a parent has died when the child is still young.

What follows is a true account, with permission, of the experiences of someone well known to the author, describing the effects of unresolved loss, and of the subsequent healing process. It leads on to the help which parents and carers can offer children in working through their grief instead of locking it inside themselves.

Maggie Kindred

1

How it began - the story of Em

Em drove slowly along a wooded road. The trees dripped with the damp, bare beauty of a January day. Her mood was flat - a glimmer of hope somewhere in the corner. She also felt apprehensive and slightly unreal. A figure stood in a welcoming pose outside a pretty cottage. Presumably this must be the person she had come to meet.

So, why was she, a fifty-six year old woman, making this journey in the middle of a working day? The answer lies near the beginning of her life.

Em was born in 1940, a wartime child of a couple whom she thinks had some trouble in conceiving, since they had been married ten years before her arrival. However, she feels sure she was welcomed into the world. How does she know? There is no evidence other than her own enjoyment of the process of pregnancy and nurturing a baby, which she believes mirrors her mother's.

A second child was born to the couple some sixteen months later in February 1942. In winter wartime, small country maternity hospitals can hardly have boasted many facilities for complicated births. Em is not entirely sure of the medical facts, but her mother died ten days after giving birth to her baby, who also did not survive.

So what might the scenario have been for the sixteen-month-old Em? It has taken her most of her lifetime to reconstruct it.

Carers and parents do their best; so when Em's mother died, first of all her maternal grandmother came to live with her and her father - a very normal strategy at that time. Em believes that this measure has the potential for either rescue or disaster, or possibly a mixture of both. Taking two shocked and bereaved adult individuals who are related only through the person they loved and lost, putting them together in a house with one or more confused and deprived children, is often a recipe for a range of difficulties which can magnify the loss they have just endured. Em intends no criticism of all loving grandparents, rather an acknowledgement of the difficulties facing them in such circumstances, when they put all their own plans on hold for contemplating or enjoying retirement. She believes her father and grandmother worked very hard for her on her behalf. Later, she learned that there were tensions between them - not very surprising since they had not chosen to live together.

Imagine then the day of her mother's death. No telephones in households of her social class; so the news would have come via her father from the hospital, or possibly by the police. Her father was a sensitive, gentleman. She has no doubt that he loved his wife Jean dearly. Jean's final letter, written from her hospital bed, which he carried in his wallet until he died, is one of the most moving communications she has ever read, and testifies to a wonderfully close relationship. So the face he showed to his daughter that terrible day can only have further destroyed her world. Em believes that young children are as affected by atmosphere as by the air they breathe. If so, she would have absorbed the two faces before her: tearful, white and drained. Her mother had already been gone for ten days. She would have been prepared for this to some extent, told that she was to have a baby sister or brother, invited to view the bump! At that stage the emotional atmosphere was likely to have been positive. However, the separation between a sixteen month old and her mother or main carer cannot be anything other than traumatic: the child simply has not got the cognitive skill to understand. So, already bruised, the toddler is told that 'Mum isn't coming back after all'. How does anyone convey such news? It is the author's experience that people either avoid saying anything, or try to find some euphemism such as 'mummy's ill' or 'mummy's gone to heaven'. The toddler may react overtly with tears to whatever she is told - more likely there will be no obvious response.

Young children's 'words' are disturbances in the basic human functions: eating, sleeping, playing and other bodily processes. When a parent or carer disappears, it is as though the young child has received a prolonged electric shock. He/she seizes up as his/her immature brain and emotions try to cope. This kind of process is now recognised as trauma, a word which until quite recently we thought of as belonging to earthquakes or accidents.

Em has no recall of any of those dark days in 1942. What she does know is that she has always been particularly uncoordinated in her ability to fit things together - a handicap in an increasingly technological age! She also finds it hard to allow herself to be creative in games which involve uninhibited self-expression. She considers herself creative in other aspects of life, so has come to the conclusion that her father and grandmother did not play with her during that vital time, so spontaneity never developed. She has every sympathy with them: it must have been quite enough of a struggle to cook, shop, keep Em warm and clean in wintry 1942, whilst trying to deal with their pain. Em thinks, as she has already indicated, that people's strategies for managing include a large element of trying to hide or suppress feelings, particularly if they are 'keeping things normal' for a young child.

Em has always been a poor sleeper. As a parent herself, she is powerfully aware of the vulnerability of the toddler at night; the need for the main carer to be there. How far Em's father had previously been the main carer is not known; however it was more usual for the mother to do the 'night watch', especially if the father was in work. She knows her cot was not in her parent's room, when she was aged two and three, as she can recall pulling off the sitting room wallpaper from the whole area within her small reach!

The young child's mechanism for dealing with pain beyond its capability is to 'blank out'. So, in spite of her grandmother being close to her for five years, and looking after her for almost four of them, she has no recollection whatsoever of her looks, words, or any incident involving her during that time. She did not search for a photo of her grandmother until she was in her fifties, and the picture evoked only the faintest recall of what must once have been a familiar face. She had been told how independent she was: would not sit on anyone's knee, and needed little attention. A highly independent child is reassuring to carers, so that they can comment with relief that he/she seems to be managing so well. Such apparent independence is possibly a dangerous sign psychologically, as Em's experience later demonstrates. All she may have been doing was making sure she was never close to anyone again.

It is true that there were factors which exacerbated this problem. Her father did not work for two years after his wife's death. While this had the advantage of giving him more time with her than usual, it is now evident that he was suffering from some form of depression. She remembers weekly walks to the doctor's surgery, some two miles away. This gave companionship, but applying the emotional thermometer of hindsight, there was a curious flat monochromatic quality to their life together. Em does not know whether her father already had a tendency towards depression before his personal tragedy hit, but it seems clear that if he had had a different emotional make-up, he would have pulled his life together more quickly. Obviously, in pre-National Health Service Britain, lack of income also had serious consequences for the family. He never recovered: throughout her childhood, he had occasional days off work, saying 'just couldn't go'. Em felt ambivalent about this: on the one hand it was comforting to have a parent at home like anyone else, but accompanying this was a sense of deep foreboding. As you might now expect, none of this could be discussed.

There was support from Em's mother's only brother and his wife, Polly. Photographs suggest that there had been close and frequent contact. However, Polly, a young woman, died when Em was only three - the second significant death.

When her grandmother left to return to her own home and die soon afterwards, Em's protective mechanisms were such that she has no memory whatsoever of this happening. In the same year, her paternal grandmother also died. Em cannot even remember her though she lived only five minutes away. Tears and need for comfort simply did not happen. Instead came a fierce independence which shrugged off all but the most basic assistance. By the time Em was five then, the scene was already set for her to manage life in an unhealthy way. It is not appropriate for a child to be trying to depend solely on herself.

Another female figure came to the rescue in the form of a paternal aunt who had been conveniently left by her sister who had married. Auntie L was an intelligent woman

whose own life had been blighted by deafness, following a measles attack. Em remembers her aunt with great affection, especially trips out with her. Visits to the seaside and the local city were the nearest she came to a 'normal' childhood. There were few visitors, and contact with other children was rare, out of school hours. The local aunts and cousin visited frequently though, and Em enjoyed this, but did not keep in contact with them when she left the home area.

The body has its own ways of dealing with trauma, and these are not always healthy. Em's digestive system seemed to seize up, so that she suffered from constipation for a large part of her life. This was severe enough to put her in hospital a few months after her auntie had come to live with her and her grandmother had left. She vaguely remembers sitting in her iron hospital bed and being told 'It`s your birthday' - her sixth - but not being particularly upset at having no visitors, cards or presents. Few people knew enough to look at emotional causes for constipation, enemas and tests being much more the norm, though exceptionally Em remembers one doctor saying 'she'll need to see a child psychologist'. The reaction to this from Aunt L was, predictably enough, horror, and it never happened. It may not have occurred to Auntie L that Em was reacting to her grandmothers' demise, as well as her mother's five years before. However Em remembers with gratitude that Auntie L dealt patiently with soiled pants, enemas and the worry of what on earth was the cause of Em having such babyish ways.

Em now realises that Auntie L may have had far more understanding than she is being given credit for. The word 'regression' wasn't in common parlance. If Auntie L intuitively comprehended Em's condition, it would not have occurred to her to communicate this to her, again compounding the conspiracy of secrecy.

Perhaps the best overall description of Em's early life was a childhood of silence. She spent much time alone, and developed strong relationships with her imaginary sister, to whom she significantly gave her mother's name, Jean. One of the best aspects of her childhood home was the animals and birds: the bullocks, hens, geese, dog and cat became her firm friends.

Contained in the silence were the innocently powerful secrets about her mother which can never now be revealed. It is possible that all families keep secrets, understandably about such subjects as serious illness or past abuse. But why do adults keep secrets from children about important loved ones? Part of the answer seems to be in the efforts to minimise pain alluded to earlier. However, experts suggest that children intuitively know that secrets are being kept from them. The room may become hushed when they enter; the topic of conversation may suddenly change when they are within earshot; inconsistencies in family stories may become apparent. Youth may not know the content of the secret, but it is very likely that they know of the secret's existence (Baker 2003).

In partnership with the secrets is the commonsense adage 'We'll tell her/him when she/he asks'. Em has tried throughout her professional life to explain to other parents that children *don't* readily ask questions which they sense are too painful for adults to deal with. Her family recognised the anguish, but could do nothing about it.

Remembering an occasion when she did ask, she estimates that she must have been nine or ten when she enquired how her mother had died. The answer was 'having a baby', which she later found was not strictly accurate, and her attitude to childbirth obviously received a setback. More positively, affectionate comments were occasionally dropped out, especially when Em reminded her father of her mother. But she grew up with no real picture. The few photos in the house were curiously enough of no interest to her during her childhood. This could only have been because the blocking out process was almost total.

Another human phenomenon seems to be the tendency of small children to feel that tragedies involving their parents are somehow their fault. Em was certainly ashamed of the fact that she had no mother, and always tried to avoid mentioning this to others. As late as seventeen, she remembers telling a boyfriend who had called unexpectedly that her mother was out.

When Em was eleven Auntie L developed cancer. Predictably, Em was told her auntie had 'appendicitis' and needed an operation. Going to stay with her uncle at his farm was some compensation. With the instinct which children have though, something told Em that there was more to the illness than appendicitis. During the stay at the farm, she remembers having a 'hysterical fit' and was described by her aunt as being 'highly strung'. Auntie L recovered and Em returned home. However the normal pattern of life was short-lived, as Auntie L succumbed to horrific pain and was finally hospitalised. When she died, Em remembers seeing the kitchen through tears, but nothing else in the way of grief: her coping strategies were by now invincible. On the day of Auntie L's funeral, she recalls being reprimanded by another aunt for asking if she had had a good day. Em was chastened at being told off for trying to be polite and social: to this day she produces tactless responses to things.

Adolescence is thought to be a period of opportunity to make up some of the deficiencies of earlier stages, not least because the young person can be fortunate enough to find some 'alternative parents', who may be relatives, parents' friends, or others.

Em was fortunate in being quite bright, so her contacts were made through her intellect. This is a well-known route for people who are not very comfortable with their emotions: thinking seems much safer than feeling.

She would like at this point to acknowledge the enormous debt she owes to her grammar school. With hindsight she has realised how unique this was: a 1930s state establishment of only 150 pupils. More pertinently, the staff comprised local people, some of whom came from working class backgrounds similar to their pupils'. In Em's later experience grammar school teachers did not live in council houses as hers did. The more memorable were those who lived by socialist principles and were responsible for the birth of these in Em; all teachers treated children with respect and wanted them to get on in life. No doubt because of this culture bullying was unheard of at least among the girls (she cannot speak for the boys). Looking back on the motherless young person she was, Em wonders how she would have survived the turbulent teenage years without the family atmosphere of her school. I wish that ex-teachers of Lemington grammar school or their children could read this.

Her first mentor was her teacher of religious education and music. A sensitive and creative woman, Miss E obviously liked to befriend. By the time she was sixteen, Em was visiting Miss E each week. With hindsight this was clearly a very guarded relationship on both sides. For instance, Em did not tell Miss E that her father had retired. It is curious that such unshameful information was held back - perhaps an example of Em's feeling that her family was deficient: no-one else's father was old enough to be retired. Miss E's influence was helpful: Em subsequently became a teacher of religious education and music herself.

Em's church contacts provided her with her next 'alternative adults', in this case a middle-aged couple. Obviously she was not at this stage conscious of searching for substitute parents, and in her fierce independence would have been affronted at the suggestion. Mollie and Len were childless, warm and caring, and vaguely related to Em. They were only too glad to take her on, and she spent many happy years in their company, even lived with them for a year when her father died. Em was fortunate that she lived in a place where such contacts could be easily made, and her church membership gave her a sense of family. Looking back, she believes that this was a large part of her salvation

Religion is a comforting and safe haven for people with emotional difficulties. This is not a judgement on its veracity; Em would prefer not to get into that debate. For her as a teenager, the search for God was satisfying and exciting. She recalls the struggle to overcome her shyness so that she could attend the early communion service, and the nurture that this provided each week. You will not be surprised to hear that Em had already developed highly structured patterns for organising her life. These have been a permanent feature, the cause of much amusement and some irritation to her friends. So during her adolescent years the week climbed to its pinnacle, the Sunday worship. The Church was both a family and a source of wonderful friends to whom she owes an enormous debt.

Spiritually she was sustained until she obtained a family of her own. At that time the sense of the reality of God began to ebb; for her it seems religion was a substitute for human love. She regrets her loss of faith, but believes that everyone's spiritual journey is different - you have to follow it honestly.

In adolescence she also began to work on self-improvement. Early targets were her speech and her behaviour. Em had learned by the time that she was thirteen that a working class background is a disadvantage. How did she know - no-one had ever criticised her accent? She thinks that awareness of disadvantage is taken in unconsciously like breathing. She had one friend who had been taken out of the state education system, and had a 'posh' accent. Em did not go so far as to emulate this, but somehow knew that she needed to speak better.

Paradoxically the aspect of Em's speech which should have been attended to was neglected. She was born with a rather small mouth, so developed a lisp and indistinct speech. No-one picked this up during her primary school years, but at grammar school the nurse referred her to the local speech therapy clinic. Her father's work precluded taking her to the appointments, and she remembers a dark, cold and uninviting first visit. Predictably, she did not turn up again. Auntie L had by this time died. Her father, she now realises, took the line of least resistance where managing Em was concerned, so she was not pressured to continue her visits. Her indistinct speech and slight lisp have subsequently proved to be a problem. This is another example of the exacerbating factors of Em's motherless state: had her father been less depressed and able to reach out to his daughter emotionally, the effects of the loss could have been mitigated.

Ostensibly, she was a carefree, sociable young person, popular with her peers and doing well enough at school to cause no concern. It was to her curious that her exam results were a mixture of highs and lows, with no in-betweens. She has later learned that this is often a symptom of emotional imbalance, and in Em's case the successful subjects were the ones which were taught by Em's 'surrogate parents'.

It has been noted by Rutter (2002) and others that young people may deal with their emotional scars by developing a 'false self' which, as in Em's case can be extremely plausible and serviceable. However, there has to be a deficit somewhere if the individual has a large chasm behind the apparently well adjusted exterior. In Em's case this began to be obvious in her sexual development. She was very frightened of peer relationships generally and tended to keep them tightly under her own control. For example, her closest girl friend once cycled two miles to see her and Em remembers hiding in the house, because for some quite unaccountable reason, she did not wish to see her that day. As far as boys were concerned, they came and went. In the 1950s full sexual relationships were not the norm, various degrees of petting were. Em can recall no sexual feelings until she was twenty-three. By then, she was well set up with friends of both sexes, some of whom are lifelong, and she is very grateful for their love and care.

Em went to college to train as a teacher. Towards the end of this period, her father developed cancer and died a few weeks after she qualified. As you will now expect, she went stoically through the illness and funeral.

However, she did grieve when he died; cried for days, and felt herself (realistically) to be alone in the world. It appears that her frozen response mechanisms had selected only mother figures; men had not let her down so far. Certainly an aunt who arrived to stay with Em immediately after the death, and for the funeral, somehow expected Em to be 'close' and criticised her for her rejecting behaviour, not wearing the right clothes, and for being 'dreamy'. It is a pity that the aunt did not have a little more knowledge of the grieving process: expecting someone like Em at that stage to be intimate was as unrealistic an expectation as making friends with a leopard.

She was, by then, twenty-two. If asked, she would have said that she had had a happy childhood. However, the effects of her loss of four female parent figures and of her father were soon to be seen in her adult relationships: the 'secrets' have a life of their own.

Next she trod the classic path of someone in her situation: she fell in love with a much older man. She was by now a committed church member, and had a job as organist and choir director. The tale of vicar and organist falling in love is almost an embarrassing cliché. However, it is necessary to look behind the lines a little: church personnel were and still are more vulnerable than other professionals because of the unstructured nature of their role. It is difficult, if not impossible, to care whilst remaining emotionally uninvolved. Therapists and others who care for people in their homes build in boundaries to protect themselves: priests sometimes do not. Em was realistically a bereaved young woman in need of support, and Colin was both her pastor and colleague. All this may look like an excuse for Em and Colin's behaviour; to this day, Em does not feel particularly guilty on her own behalf, nor condemnatory of Colin. In a sense very little happened: Colin called frequently at the cottage, and after nine months someone called his wife to say that Colin was 'associating with a young woman'. Informers of wives may not be aware of how they can fan a flame which was almost non-existent before they took action. Certainly Em was completely unaware to the point of naivety, a word which has been used about her from time to time by both her friends and enemies so that she wonders if it is part of her legacy of loss.

The revelation that Colin's wife had been informed initiated the most turbulent period of Em's life. This lasted four months and comprised two outings and one kiss. The kiss was enough for Em to realise she was a sexual person after all, and the second of the two outings was probably the highlight of her life to date. Following the kiss, Colin very sensibly and bravely cut the contact with Em altogether. For her, the agony which followed was well nigh unbearable. As she was well versed in carrying on regardless, she turned up at her job each day, cried all night, and so the time went on. To say she 'moved on' emotionally, unfortunately would not be accurate: having actually engaged with someone, she could not let go of him for a good ten years. Nevertheless, it was for her essentially a healing experience, in spite of the negative outcome. Colin was a sensitive, creative and deeply caring man who had pulled back from the brink of abusing Em. He explained that he could not either give up his vocation or leave his wife; this she completely accepted. The excruciating pain, which can only be understood by someone who has loved and lost, was positive in the sense that it represented life and engagement rather than staying safe in an emotional fortress. Her close friends supported her wonderfully, and encouraged her to move house.

The next few years covered the development of her career, first in teaching, then social work. Helping others is often a vocational choice for those who have had emotional turmoil in their own lives. In Em's case it was constructive, not least because the training introduced her to aspects of herself which she had not encountered before, in the previously locked cupboards containing the memories of her mother. It did not take a perceptive tutor long to 'diagnose' Em's problem. She commented that Em recited the story of her losses 'just like a shopping list'. Em was mystified: how else should she describe them? So her condition was apparent to the trained observer, but not at this stage understood by her. She found the training useful and qualified as a social worker when she was twenty-nine. However this self development brought the first periods of depression, apparently without cause. Depression felt quite different from the stark agony she had endured following her broken heart.

Em gradually broadened her experience. The eight years she subsequently spent in London were her happiest professional years. She had a good social life and enjoyed the multi-cultural and stimulating environment she found there. If it were not for the aching need she felt for a life partner, she would have been fulfilled. As in adolescence, men friends came and went without anything significant ensuing.

As her thirties progressed, Em reached some sort of peace with herself, entering what for many people become the increasingly contemplative years. Along with this was a sense that her biological clock was marching on. Watching her friends marry and have children had taught her, she thought, that she was not up to being a parent. She was aware of something sadly lacking when she watched others handling the more taxing aspects of their toddlers' behaviour. Later she found this elusive something defined by childcare experts as 'the ability to put the child's needs before one's own'. It fits the bill. Professionally, she related best to older children and adolescents. Babies she loved, but the toddler and young child seemed to demand something from her she had not in her to give. She believes that her deficiencies and strengths relate directly to the times in her life when she had either been neglected or nurtured. By thirty-six, ostensibly she was happier, yet paradoxically searching for a solution to her problems before it was too late, because behind the conscious ache for a partner was the submerged need for a child. So, as has been the case with many of her most important decisions, Em suddenly found herself proposing a course of action without apparently having thought about it: 'I think I'll go into therapy'. The secrets were not to be left undisturbed.

The beginnings of surfacing the grief

Most people are driven to therapy because they are in pain. There is also a need to feel generally safe enough to undertake the process. Em was in less conscious pain than at other points in her life by her mid thirties. She spoke vaguely to friends and colleagues about wanting therapy for 'personal development', but she knew perfectly well that she wanted a partner very badly and therapy seemed a way to help. You may well be thinking that computer dating (the internet was not in popular use in the mid-seventies) would have been cheaper and more efficient! It is necessary here to understand Em's deeply introspective and analytical mindset at that time: she thought of almost all problems as coming from self and that self could solve them, if anyone could. The proverbial biological clock was also ticking loudly:

although Em could not see herself as a mother, part of her badly wanted to be one.

At this point the author would like to acknowledge the difficult process of entering into therapy. First there are societal attitudes: that people in therapy need to be mentally ill, that they are mad, that they are self indulgent and need to 'pull themselves together'. Secondly there is the confusing language: counselling, psychoanalysis, cognitive therapy; to mention only a few of the words which swirl round. Thirdly there is the process and potential expense of finding someone. Finally, therapy is a step which needs courage to venture into the unknown.

Em was fortunate that her job and contacts gave her some understanding of the ideas behind the process. She was aware that, at that time, there was something of a minefield, that anyone could put up a plate outside their door announcing themselves as a therapist. To that extent public fears were very much justified: now there is very much more regulation of practitioners, though it is still by no means foolproof. As Em had the means to pay, the choice of route and practitioners was easy for her:

Everything Em had ever read or heard about therapy suggested that the rapport between the client and therapist is the most important element. So she was pleased to find Diane, an experienced therapist who seemed to her to be both kind and firm. What follows is the essence of six months of working together for three hourly sessions per week.

Em told Diane her life story. As had happened before when some of her tutors and supervisors had found out how many significant adults had died in her childhood, Em was slightly irritated to find how much attention Diane paid to the deaths, and the bad effects these must have had. It is normal to defend oneself against pain, so all therapists recognise that it will take time and patience to help their clients to face what is sometimes near unbearable pain. So Em spent weeks telling Diane about work, how she would love a partner in her life, describing incidents past and present, and generally having a stimulating and intellectually challenging time.

The relationship with a therapist is gradually constructed by the building blocks of small, everyday incidents, which assume massive proportions at the time. Two such spring to mind. Em visited Diane in the early morning, when there was often some recently delivered milk on Diane's doorstep. Em used at first to pick up the milk bottles and hand them to Diane, until she was gently asked not to by Diane who said she felt 'taken over 'by Em doing this. The second incident was when Diane asked Em to stop talking when her time had run out at the end of the session. Both insignificant happenings caused Em inordinate pain: she cried all the way to work each time. Unlike the misconception that therapists' break people down' in order, presumably to put them together again, the therapeutic process requires the client to risk a state of extreme vulnerability, when the normal protective layers are discarded. Good therapists never force or bully, but allow the client to be in control, and the process to happen, rather like a cake cooking in the oven, which cannot be hurried without spoiling it. To take this analogy a little further: just as the cake will also spoil if the oven is too cool, competent therapists do not allow their clients so easy a time that they make no progress or become bored.

A milestone came at the end of the summer holidays. Em and Diane had been separated for several weeks. The evening before sessions resumed, Em was wondering why she was in therapy, it seemed a waste of time and money, how was she to extricate herself? Then came a phone call from Diane saying that she was sorry that she could not make the next morning's session. Em was heartbroken; felt she would do anything to be able to attend her session. Such is the nature of what psychiatrists call defences: the link between Em and Diane had been (unavoidably) damaged by the holiday, but Em's need of Diane surfaced immediately when the link was threatened.

The link continued to wobble when Diane told Em that she has been diagnosed with a serious, though not life-threatening illness. She tended to steer clear of anyone who was ill if at all possible. Nevertheless, the sessions continued, and Em began to understand intellectually how devastating it was for a small child to lose a mother, with little attempt on the part of alternative adults to keep that mother alive.

Em could not believe her good fortune when she met Andrew while she was in therapy- was this a coincidence? Diane helped her not to opt out of the relationship, which she could easily have done, because of her fear of being close to anyone. It became a partnership of a quality beyond her wildest dreams.

The intellectual knowledge she had gained in therapy did not itself achieve lasting change. Her work with Diane ended on grounds of cost and perceived 'no need' - she had someone to love her by now. But the 'grief unobserved' had left deep scars.

Her partner seemed to have had a good experience as a young child. This reassured Em and helped her to take the risk of trying for a child, whom she wanted very much. She was fortunate in having a relatively trouble-free pregnancy and birth, though was quite happy to be counselled out of trying for another baby - since she certainly did not want to follow in the path of her own mother - their ages were almost identical.

Em's child was a sunny, gifted little girl - a great joy to her. However, she was conscious of the feeling of 'a big gap somewhere' from time to time. What was also happening, although she was not aware of it at the time, was that Em was giving too much of her emotional energy to her work. It is possible to feel far more adequate in 'helping others' than in close relationships at home.

Nevertheless, doubtless by a combination of genes, an adequate father figure, and goodwill, Em's daughter grew up poised, generous and caring, and a relationship developed in adulthood which the two women found mutually supportive – even in helping each other with their work - an enormous bonus! But before this positive outcome there was a crisis of enormous proportions.

When Em was fifty-six she had everything she had ever wanted, and more: partner, daughter, career and home. So how could she have become at this stage depressed, suicidal, dreading the retirement which was on the horizon, and letting her partner and daughter down? She regularly told herself that a 'good kick in the pants' was what was necessary. The trouble was that such strictures did not work, as is often the case. So, reluctantly because it seemed such a monstrous self-indulgence, she had chosen to consult a psychotherapist, and was travelling anxiously along the country road to meet her.

2

Grief unobserved is treated

It began with the job not going particularly well. Em felt undervalued by her employers because she had so many underlying needs, the approbation of bosses was particularly important to her, and managers vary in their willingness or ability to give this kind of support. She became depressed: much worse than on previous occasions during early adulthood. What was she to do when she retired? What was there to look forward to? Her condition was made worse by the knowledge that she had everything she ever wanted out of life and a lot more. Depressed people often feel that 'they need a kick in the pants' even if others are not giving them this message. Things became so bad that Em agreed to go into therapy again. A friend suggested someone suitable.

In this book the word therapy is used in its simplest form. It encompasses the kind of help which any sensitive adult can offer. However, there are aspects which need training as well as skill and commitment. These are referred to in the account of Em's therapy, but in essence an *experience* is being described rather than treatment methods.

Beginning

Em brought with her an enormous amount of apprehension, even though she had been in therapy before. It felt akin to anticipating a major physical operation, which in a way, it was. The therapist stood outside her house to meet her - a helpful touch. Em saw a beautiful woman with a sensitive facial expression. The therapy room was something of a revelation, in that it was furnished with two low couches facing each other. Both parties could sit, sprawl or lie down among a pile of cushions. Em had always been taught that it was best to sit in an oblique position in any kind of counselling work, so that the client did not have to face the helper if he/she did not want to.

Introductions, recording of details and making a working agreement went conventionally - except that Em found herself asking far too many personal questions of her therapist - her face burns in shame at this recall. All clients test the therapist out in some way. In Em's case there may have already been a need to find out information in much the same matter-of-fact way as does a young child. She later called her therapist 'Taffy', having discovered some Welsh connections. Taffy showed her competence by her intuitive understanding of Em - many therapists would have refused to answer personal questions.

'A honeymoon'

As Em was in such a broken-up state, it was curious that she seemed to feel better very quickly: she thinks this can only have been because she had found someone whom she knew had the competence to help her. Those early days were notable for Taffy's remarks and responses which were unlike anyone else in her experience. She was asked to keep a therapy diary, which Taffy patiently read between sessions. The latter had already explained that her type of therapy needed the client's face to be seen clearly, hence the seating arrangement. She also said that Em's problem could not be solved quickly. The first three months felt like a wonderful journey of self discovery -to some extent going over the old ground of Em's life story and her previous therapy. Life seemed rich and full again. Husband and friends were rather bemused at the remarkable recovery!

Digging deeper

Em had already found herself losing her usual inhibitions and fierce independence. Then she started to feel very strongly that she wanted Taffy to take the initiative. Again, this does not sound like conventional therapy, where the client is always encouraged to take the initiative - but it is always so individual that most general principles become meaningless. Here, with hindsight, it seems to Em that she was trying to undo some of the independence she had taken on, far too young, as a way of coping. One striking example: she and Taffy decided to make an album containing all the photographs and momentos which she possessed of her early life. To her later embarrassment, Em found herself asking Taffy to buy the album for her, to which Taffy readily agreed. The impertinence of it! The album was duly bought, and Em was pleased to see that it had discreet hearts on the cover design, and that Taffy had written 'with love from...' (her real name at this stage.

Easter realities

It was on Easter Sunday, when a friend who was staying with Em, remarked during the church service that Easter tended to bring people's losses into their consciousness. Em cried and cried throughout the service. Hitherto, she had been something of a weepy person, but always if someone hurt her, never to do with death. A few days later she woke in the night with a mixture of tears and hysterical laughter. She did wonder if she were going mad, but knew the therapy was in fact beginning to reach the parts which had been locked away.

Here Em feels it is worth leaving the chronological passage of the therapy and describe some important features for someone whose problem is unresolved grief.

Good touching

A young child's distress can be so deeply buried that it is virtually unreachable except through therapy, when normal defences against pain are gradually relinquished. When the therapy is about the reparation of someone who has experienced loss as a young child, touch is possibly the most important element - 'it is the mother of the senses' (Montagu 1986, p. 17).

You will recall that Em had managed to achieve a happy marriage. By the time of her therapy she had had almost twenty years of 'good touching' in her everyday life. Why was this not enough? Possibly because it needed Em to be so horribly exposed and vulnerable within therapy - therapeutic touch is of a different order than a husband's. One of the reasons that Taffy was so right for Em was that her original training had included the use of 'physical techniques'. More importantly she was warm and responsive as a person.

So it was that, five months into the therapy, Taffy suggested that at some point in their work together, it might be helpful if she left her couch on the other side of the room and joined Em on hers, so that there would be the chance of physical contact. Em's immediate response was a mixture of intuitive wariness and a strong sense of trust in Taffy. Also she had always been the kind of person to respond to a proffered challenge. So she invited Taffy to join her, feeling very embarrassed, incoherent, and uncomfortable. Like others whose capacity for intimacy has been damaged, her immediate response included fear of 'smelling' despite a recent shower, worrying about 'doing the right thing', instead of relaxing into the experience. Taffy took hold of Em's hand, producing a heightened response similar to a sexual one. Taffy asked how Em felt - Em said, again to her own considerable embarrassment 'I think you are very beautiful'. The rest of the session was concerned with Taffy helping Em to calm down, stay still and relax. From that point on, Taffy continued to ask Em at the beginning of each session if she wanted her to join her, and there was much cuddling and comforting during the painful middle phase of the therapy. Towards the end it was natural for Taffy to withdraw again to her own side of the room.

Note

The use of touch in therapy has obviously always been complex, since it is so primal, powerful and the feelings it arouses are impossible to detach conclusively from sexuality. In recent years the therapist's task has been made more difficult by our growing awareness of sexual abuse in general, and even abuse of both children and adults by professionals. However some trained professionals risk using touch under clinical supervision.

Some experts maintain that we cannot thrive as infants without being touched (Field 1995). This may be a theory that you cannot prove or disprove, but it is worth remembering that many of us have been short of good touching during our lifetime. You will recall that Em refused to be touched in her early years if at all possible.

Play

Em had missed out on some vital input from adults - being played with when she was a toddler. So Taffy encouraged her to touch and cuddle the toys in the room, to take some home with her, and to talk to them in her diary. This was the part which was least fruitful for Em - the process felt artificial and perfunctory. She did, however, enjoy painting and drawing some scenes from her childhood. She concludes that she was badly damaged in this respect - to this day really only enjoys games with an intellectual content. The fact that she has so little to say about this part of the therapy also speaks volumes.

Gathering information

Life story books were developed to help children who had lost touch with their original families and roots, but provide an excellent opportunity for a person of any age to piece together their past. Em's album progressed during this time. Six months into her therapy she revisited her birthplace, looked at her mother's grave, and put such information together as she already had.

One of the problems was that she had left it so late in her life that there were few people left who had known her mother. However she collected everything:

Recollections from talking to her father - 'Mum's first Sunday lunch was a disaster: she ended up with all the dishes on the floor beside the oven'.

'She got hurt; I kept telling her not to get involved with all those cliques at the church, but she wouldn't listen'.

From her cousins - 'She wore corsets so tight on a theatre visit with your Dad that she fainted and finished up in the manager's office'. 'She never stopped talking and laughing; no-one got any sleep if they shared a room with her'.

From a dear friend- 'She loved shopping and being nicely dressed'. 'She tended to break all her nice china and simply got on the bus to town and bought some more'.

From her well loved cousin who is the only family member she is in touch with - 'She was refined, very sensitive and happy'.

'I was 12 at the time she died. Em, you were wild and completely untouchable '.

Most telling of all: 'I've told you all this before, you know - you didn't want to know'.

She felt it was uncanny how like her mother she seemed: chocaholic, awful hair, love of colour, homemaking, clothes, piano playing and shopping. Of course no one told her any negative things, making her mother somewhat unreal.

'Therapeutic ECT'

Soon after the summer break Taffy suggested Em take some time off work. This idea was absolutely *unthinkable*, Em being the kind of person who had only 2 days off in 30 years, and took pride in plodding grimly on, however bad she felt physically or mentally, and no doubt scattering cold germs everywhere from time to time!

However she soon agreed, under her self-made rule that Taffy should 'be in charge'. To her surprise her doctor signed her off for a month with hardly a murmur- she must have by this time looked terribly depressed.

Small incidents are very important in therapy, and four happened in close succession: Taffy (who actually was human!) forgot a session, Em developed one of those sudden agonizing back conditions, and her doctor told her off for not taking the anti-depressants he had prescribed.

Then Em had asked Taffy to come to her home if she could not drive because of her back, and Taffy had refused.

So Em dragged herself off to the session, angry, disheartened, and feeling very sorry for herself: 'What on earth is the point of spending all this on therapy, it's far too late, Taffy doesn't care anyway, and my doctor doesn't understand that medication will undermine the therapy'.

It got worse: Taffy seemed cold and distant, didn't seem to care about Em's inability to sit on such a low chair, only offered one tissue, and appeared unsympathetic about the doctor's attitude. Through the gallons of tears Em heard Taffy being cross about Em saying the therapy was no good, giving her advice about her back condition, and criticising her for not making eye contact. At one point Taffy actually ordered Em to look at her, which to her own amazement, she actually did. She asked when Em was going to risk being properly angry and that she lashed out at people, did she not? Em felt that her faults were being thrown in her face.

There were three islands in this sea of tears:

Em almost smiled when Taffy, whom she had never heard swear, said 'Cut out the crap Em...my heart goes out to you in this process'.

Brokenly, during discussion of the therapy process, Em asked 'What is playing with teddies about then, Taffy?' She answered 'I had to give you an experience of what you'd missed so that you would feel the loss. You can play with the teddies any time you like'. This suddenly made absolute sense to Em, and without it she does not feel she would have coped.

Towards the end of the session Taffy said, 'If you would but know it, you're doing very well'. Though she answered ungraciously, Em was pathetically grateful for this piece of encouragement.

She got through the day somehow, and cried most of the next two days and nights. It seemed that she must be so horrible that even the kindest and most understanding people rejected her in the end. What now? The time to return to work was very near- therapy had not 'worked', she had deprived her family of substantial amounts of money, and was 'a mess.' Now she was crying for the loss of Taffy as well as all the others.

Weakened states sometimes bring revelations, this perhaps why ascetics fast. The dawn of the third day brought a bombshell: *Taffy had made her suffer for a purpose - to feel the loss in all its agony. It was almost as simple as that. Her skill as a therapist enabled her to take the risk of Em opting out. It would have been useless for Em to mourn Taffy after she had left therapy - there was still much to do*

Em had a lovely day, in spite of no sleep, swollen eyes and bad back. She had a few days before going back to work - the crisis had no doubt timed itself with this in mind.

She wrote in her diary 'Don't worry Taffy, I don't think I'm cured'.

Memorial

Rituals are very important in our lives, to mark the important milestones, particularly birth, death and marriage. Em does not wish to enter the debate of whether children should attend funerals or not - but it goes without saying that, at sixteen months, her mother's would have been meaningless.

Taffy suggested that Em prepared a memorial for her mother, which would include a 'What I would like to say to you' reading, specially chosen music, and small refreshments.

For the reading, Em prepared her information she had about her mother, including parts of the last letter her mother had written to her father, so full of love and feeling, and a few of her own reflections about the quality of that love. It concerned Em a little that her father went to pieces after his loss - her professional reading had taught her that failure to recover is not necessarily the mark of a positive relationship lost, more that he may have been unduly dependent.

She mentioned all the household articles which she was enjoying using in her own home - the coffee set, glass candlesticks and photos in particular. Finally, she chose music from Faure's Requiem and some 1930s dance numbers.

The preparation was all - the memorial session itself something of an anti-climax. However, it was an example of just how imaginative therapy can be - probably there are others as wonderful as Taffy but never in Em's eyes!

Ending and beginning

The therapy entered a new phase - there was much more discussion of current issues, planning for the future and anticipating an ending, though this was not put into words for about six months.

Taffy produced the last of her wonderful surprises by offering to visit Em at home, with a final session afterwards. The drink in the garden was relaxed and enjoyable. Taffy had great sense of fun, and Em's partner easily became part of the group. The last session was sad but appropriate. Em promised that she would write about her therapy and about how carers could help a child in her situation.

So what of Em's continuing life? She faced up to retirement, and gradually a new career emerged - writing training material! She remains oversensitive, but the overwhelming and disabling depression has not recurred after fifteen years of life's normal ups and downs. She will be eternally grateful, first to her partner, friends and daughter, and finally to Taffy, for their love and understanding.

3

What can be done to help?

Understanding loss

Losing one parent whilst still having the other, if there are other loving family members around the toddler, does not seem to rank among the more desperate situations in which a child could find herself. So Em never looked back on her childhood as being unhappy or saw herself as a person needing emotional assistance, nor that the help she later needed would be so radical.

However, childhood loss is perhaps more complicated than we think. Can it be the case that:

> ... *the mother- child bond is so primal we equate its severing with a child's emotional death. Everyone carries to adulthood a child's fear of being left alone. The motherless child symbolises a darker less fortunate self ..... to openly acknowledge her loss would be to acknowledge the same potential for oneself.*

(Edelmann, 1994, p. xxiii).

However, one of Em's main lessons from therapy was that it was not so much the loss that was the disaster in her life, but the way the adults had dealt with it. This is actually a very useful thing to know - that it is not inevitable that adult depression must follow childhood bereavement.

Supposing Em's father and grandmother had had different experiences themselves of being helped to cope with loss, or had received education about this, they may have been better equipped to help Em.

It had already been concluded by experts such as Bettelheim (1950) that parenting is more complicated than just loving your children, hence his book 'Love is not enough'. He advocated 'central persons' in the child's school life to complement the parents, which Em was lucky to find.

Em wishes to acknowledge at this point both the excellent work of experts who have been such splendid pioneers in children's work, and gifted, unsung individuals who have intuitively handled children's loss of carers with unerring effectiveness and skill. She has met many such. However, she believes *accurate,* as opposed to well-meaning, sensitivity to children is not yet the norm, far less in 1942. So she hopes to bring some expert knowledge to the consciousness of carers, both professional and family, who have not yet had the chance to consider it.

Love is not enough - the themes of helping

Human development and trauma

Note: 'Trauma' is used in this book to denote an unanticipated exceptional event that is powerful and dangerous in which a feeling of helplessness overwhelms the child's capacity to cope (Rice and Groves 2005).

For understanding why Em was so badly affected by her carers' silence, the starting point has to be our knowledge of the young child. Though the importance of early experience, for example in Bowlby (1969), has been challenged, as being difficult to prove, most people would agree that the child cannot deal with life like an adult.

At age 9 months - 3 years, whether because of bereavement or any other reason, the young child's vulnerability makes the caregiver's prolonged absence traumatic. Even the temporary absence of a mother at the age of 9 months has a detrimental effect. Bowlby (1973) was convincingly detailed about the two and a half year old who could not recognise her mother after only a fortnight's separation, and who grew up as an angry and depressed adult. Children look for their mother in the place she last appeared. If she does not come, the confusion increases (Edelman 1994).

For many years, the assumption was that young children could not remember trauma; therefore, it did not affect them. But Mongillo et al. (2009) found that younger children exposed to

trauma while their brains are rapidly developing are more inclined to develop post-traumatic stress disorder (PTSD), with symptoms that last longer and are more severe than adults.

Children learn to react to situations by observing and imitating the adults in their family, so Em would have picked up cues about keeping quiet about distressing events, whilst the faces round her gave a very different and frightening message. So when she became a parent herself, she had a strong feeling that she was not up to it. When her friends had children she was aware of what she could only describe as a 'blankness' where the necessary tolerance and patience for young children should have been. However, babies and adolescents were excluded from this rather dreadful, difficult to describe, lack in herself. She is sure that this was because she had

had sixteen very good months of mothering, and had managed to find helpful alternative adults in the teenage years, so had belatedly learned some good reactions The positive side of her inadequacy was that she could easily understand the parents and young people she worked with, whose behaviour was sometimes bizarre or incredibly selfish.

Understanding reactions to loss

Young children's 'words' are often expressed in their basic human functions: eating, sleeping, playing and bodily processes, so when a parent or carer disappears, it is as though the young child has received a prolonged electric shock. He/she seizes up as his/her immature brain and emotions try to cope. Juri and Marrone (2003) marked out constipation, sleep disturbance, marked withdrawal and lack of physical co-ordination continuing into later childhood as typical of the person bereaved in infancy. Em experienced them all.

Recent work by experts may have thrown further light on the young child's ways of coping with experience which is intolerable for his/her stage of development. Quite simply, the young child 'forgets'. *Forgetting is an adaptive response to the horrors of life.* (Bear 1998, p. 68).

However, somewhere between 18 months and 24 months a toddler will begin to show that he/she can think about things that aren't present. For example, the child will no longer be confused if you hide an object and then move it to another spot when she or he is looking away. After she discovers it's not where she thought it was, she'll keep searching. So you can expect the child to go on looking for her dead parent in the place where he/she was last or habitually seen. Rather than trying to stop the child's search, this is the chance to repeat gently that the parent won't be here any more, as many times as it takes, reinforcing that '----------- is here to look after you now'.

Expect that such children may have tantrums more often, either as a way to get their own sadness out, or as a reaction to the tension and grief in your household.

On the other hand, being quiet and not appearing to be distressed is a way of coping which works, and superficially it makes life easier for adults. But it is ultimately detrimental, because it can develop into a pattern of independence which is ultimately inhuman. You will recall that Em was 'wild and totally unreachable' as a toddler. Throughout her life she found the acceptance of comfort from others, even those she loved best, very difficult. When she was ill she would talk of buying a caravan and retiring like a wounded animal. The barrier needs to be breached, therefore, and the manner of this is crucial. You can't force yourself on a child, but you can keep telling her /him that you love her/him, and that you wish you could see Mummy too but you can't. Expressing your own emotions is also an important communication with the child. Explain to him that grownups need to cry, too, and that you're sad because you miss Mummy. The child is keenly aware of changes in your mood, and he'll be even more worried if he/she senses that something is wrong but that you're trying to hide it.

Expect the subject to come up repeatedly. Be ready to field the same questions from the child over and over again, since understanding the permanence of death is a real struggle. Don't worry that you didn't explain the death adequately the first time — the child's ongoing questions are normal. Just keep answering them as patiently as you can.

The wider environment

Em started, as we all do, as a member of a particular culture. A summary of what some people do in Britain goes something like this:

a) encourage the bereaved person to cry - helpful

b) try to cheer the bereaved person up or 'take him/her out of himself/herself' - can help but can fail or make the person feel worse

c) organise a mourning ceremony, religious or otherwise - usually helpful

d) celebrate the person's life - helpful

e) give the bereaved person 'time to get over it' - helpful so long as the time given is not limited

f) consult a doctor or attend counseling - sometimes referrals are made too early - grief is normal not pathological - if someone is disabled to the point of non-functioning medical or psychological intervention may be necessary.

This is not an exhaustive list, but perhaps includes some of the main themes.

It will be noted that there is nothing so far specifically for children, particularly young children. If there were anything, it would possibly be along the lines of 'keep things as normal as possible': a sensible adage. For the sixteen-month old, this means giving lots of playful stimulation as well as meals and bedtime being at times he/she is used to. The toddler can create some mental pictures at this stage, e.g. if you say you are going to the shops together, he/she remembers what this means, unless it is a first visit.

Carers' communication

Researchers find that the quality of parenting in the first 2-3 years of life is particularly important to healthy development, and the child's subsequent ability to regulate stress and emotional arousal (Schore and McIntosh 2011).

Even if this seems an extreme view, few people would disagree that hostility between carers gives a negative message to a young child. Dealing with this aspect has received much attention in relation to parents who have split up. But what about 'kinship carers?' where In many situations, as in Em's, a relative steps in, perhaps out of a sense of duty, putting his/her previous life on hold. It is hard to believe that it would be a path the grandparent, aunt or cousin would have actively chosen. It could be a worse situation than when marital partners who are now in conflict, can at least remember making a conscious commitment to each other. Em thought, as she grew older, that there were distinct tensions between her father and his wife's family, based on social class - her father hinted that 'he wasn't good enough for her'. So it is important to recognize that the adults have large mountains to climb when they take on a bereaved child: trying to cope with their own grief, the child's, plus any 'luggage' in the way of relationship problems.

However, differences in carers and caring styles are normal, and children will have their own unique experiences with each adult. By respecting their own differences, carers teach their children an important lesson on empathy and responding to individual differences in others.

It is important to protect and shield the child from being exposed to carer conflicts. The adults' greatest need is for help and support from friends or professionals.

As soon as the child is old enough he/she should have it explained that Dad and Nan sometimes disagree, and that this is not his or her fault. In the bereavement situation it is fatally easy to give a negative message, because, in a sense, the problem does centre round the child. But if the child believes that the fighting is about him or her, it will cause huge amounts of stress. Remember that children can overhear conversations extremely well even if they are out of sight. Phone conversations are especially vulnerable.

Counselling skills

Therapists are trained in techniques which enable them to listen, draw out, respond to and move forward their clients. However everyone can benefit from some training in communication skills - using these does not draw us into interpreting people's words, dreams or art work, simply makes us more effective and sensitive in ordinary life.

Here is a list of some of the more important communication skills:

1) Adopt an attitude, posture and facial expression which conveys to the other person that you want to hear what they are saying.

2) Listen 'between the lines'. As important as the actual words spoken by children or adults is the quality of voice, such as loud, soft, confident, tearful, angry, or different from their usual style.

3) Make a mental note of key words or phrases. For example, you may notice that a particular word or phrase is being repeated from time to time – ask yourself if it has any significance.

4) Make sure that you are hearing what the person

has actually said, and not what you want to hear. A lot of processing of what our ears pick up takes place in the brain when we listen to what people are saying, especially when we are emotionally close to them. For example, when a child says 'I don't want to talk about it', don't assume that they do, really. Taking the statement at face value reduces the pressure and the child is more likely to open up now or at some other time. This is not the same as Em's case, where adults were relieved at her apparent wish to back off any mention of her mother, and did not raise the matter again. You keep raising it in a casual sort of way: 'You look good wearing that colour - your mother looked nice in it too'.

5) Summarising or reflecting is a useful skill to show that you are listening and to check that you understand. For example: 'You seem to be saying that you would like…' The person then has the chance to change any misperceptions on your part.

6) Use small silences between conversations. These help the other person to reflect, compose his or her response, and create a sense of calm. Don't overdo it – about 3–10 seconds is enough. Assess the quality of the silence: it is not neutral – does it feel angry, threatening, sad, reflective, relaxed, encouraging…?

7) Recognize when questioning is useful, for example, when you need precise information, you need to open up an area, or you need to prompt. There are four main types of question:

- open questions e.g. 'And then what happened?'

- closed questions e.g. 'Do you prefer tea or coffee?'

- leading questions e.g. 'What annoys you about X?'
- probing questions e.g. 'How do you feel?'

You will be aware of some of these types of questions being used inappropriately and insensitively, e.g. when a television interviewer asks someone who has just lost a loved one 'How do you feel?'

Avoid 'why' questions – this is the language of the interrogation room. Those of us who are parents will recognize the tendency, at the end of a long hard day, to scream at

a child, 'Why did you do that?' We rarely get a useful answer!

Finally, on this subject, try not to ask too many questions.

Communicating specifically with children

Although we know that children are different from adults, we often slip into an adult way of working with them - perhaps because we do not know any other way to do it.

Working with children Bayliss (1998, p. 30 ff)

1) Make sure there is plenty to play with in the room you usually use. Include at least one doll - male or female.

2) Move to the child's level, physically. Kneel on the floor rather than sit on a chair.

3) Try to switch off your own agenda. Even a short time which is totally dedicated to the child can be effective

4) Pick up on what you sense the child is feeling: Use a doll by picking it up, giving it a cuddle, and

saying something like 'I think Teddy feels sad sometimes, because Mummy is not here'. Don't worry if there is no response. You can repeat the same procedure next time, with variations as necessary, e.g. 'I think teddy feels better today - perhaps because he knows we are looking after him'.

5) Use something special associated with the lost person: food, an item of clothing, a photo. Just talk about the chosen momento: 'This was your Mum's favourite chocolate,' 'Your Dad loved this car when he was your age'.

6) Sometimes, for the school-age child or teenager, playing a board game is a useful bridge. Game playing is not a waste of time but a necessary preliminary in such instances.

    It is the time together which matters, and the fact that you can talk about the deceased person.

7) Make visual materials age-appropriate. For example, do not give children's pictures to an adult.

8) Use a child's chosen venue for important conversations. A car journey can be good because both of you are facing forward, and a crowded bus, may be the child's choice because he/she does not feel so exposed as in the home. Don't say' We'll talk about this later', unless confidentiality is absolutely crucial.

Communicating specifically about the loss to the pre-verbal child

Making eye contact is very important when chatting to your child of 18 months to 2 years. You will remember that Taffy made a point of this in therapy. So position yourself in a way that ensures you are able to make intense eye contact.

It also helps to be aware that being able to understand a lot more than one can say can also be a significant source of frustration for both toddlers and carers at this age. The child understands your instruction, perhaps, but can't explain his/her reason for not carrying it out!

Children may believe that the deceased still eat, sleep, and do normal things — except that they do them up in the sky or down in the ground.

Young children hear words literally, therefore religious explanations that may comfort an adult may unsettle a child. For example, the explanation' Mummy is with God now,' or 'It is God's will', could be frightening rather than reassuring to the young child who may worry that God might decide to come and get her just as He did her mother. Some carers can be equally confused: for example the young mother who had just lost her five-year-old asked, in utter bewilderment, 'Why did the vicar say that Jesus wanted Mary for an angel?'

Young children can't cope with too much information at once. They can't yet grasp the concept of 'forever', and instead see death as something that's temporary and reversible. At this age, it's most helpful to explain in terms of not being able to be with the deceased any more, rather than launching into a complicated discussion. In this context, it is vitally important to help a 2-year-old understand who is going to take care of him/her.

The picture is further complicated by the young child's inability to tell us about it later. It has been suggested that the average age of the first memories is three years, six months, with the vast majority of subjects dating their first recollection somewhere between ages two and five years (Carroll 2008, p.64). Additionally, this recall is for *everyday* events, not horrible atmospheres which are totally beyond the child's comprehension.

Touch

The importance of touch has been outlined in the account of Em's therapy. You may have reservations about using it with vulnerable and damaged children, especially if you are a foster or residential carer. Your organisation may actively forbid you to use it - such has been the effect of so much sexual abuse having been exposed. One answer is to ensure you are not alone with a child when using touch. It does not have to mean cuddling - even hand holding as used by Taffy with Em has been described by one author (Knable 1981) as a means of transcending barriers of communication. It 'triggers a multitude of emotional and physical associations' (Hunter and Struve 1998, p. 8) and so can aid the memory.

This book can provide no real answer to your individual situation, except to reassert that being touched in a warm and comforting way is the key to forming close relationships later in life. Warm touching means that the world's all right in spite of the trauma; lack of touching, the opposite. At worst, lack of touch can result in the failure to thrive.

The bereaved young child can angrily shrug off the carer's attempts to comfort her, as did Em. In any case the adult is hurting enough himself/herself without trying to force physical contact on someone. Instead, he/she can use every possible opportunity: bedtime, when s/he's fallen over, when s/he's being difficult, and all the opportunities to cuddle which present themselves during the toddler's day.

Memory chest

You will recall that Em's father got rid of every single reminder of her mother, possibly to ease his own pain, as well as suppressing Em`s. She has learned that there was a large portrait of her mother in the home's main bedroom; this was disposed of, along with most of her personal possessions. If her mother had been 'kept alive' by mementoes being regularly shown to Em, along with information about her parents' life together, she may not have buried her pain so deeply. Buried distress tends to 'cause a smell in the cellar' as one thinker put it.

What helps is to do the exact opposite - collect every possible momento. Em did this later in her therapy, but her mother's memory should have been everywhere around her childhood home: in photos, pictures, clothes, special belongings as well as the household objects which did give her a flavour of her mother's tastes and personality.

The specific treasure chest may be brought out from time to time. In addition, a life story book or album can include all the details of pregnancy, birth, previous homes if the family has moved, the significant adults and carers who helped out, what the parents enjoyed doing together and separately, food preferences and holidays.

If the child appears not to want to know, as did Em when taken to see her mother's grave, just choose another momento and another moment. Exactly as an adopted child needs to grow up with the knowledge of his/her roots, the bereaved child needs to deepen her picture of hers from the beginning. She needs to know about her mother's weaknesses as well as her strengths. Giving a child painful information on a specific day, at a specific age is simply not on - the recollections of so many adopted children tell us how their world was destroyed by such practice.

The bonus of the 'treasure chest' approach is that it helps the carers as much as the child. If the original bereavement has been more knowledgeably handled, Em would perhaps not have needed to 'forget' her grandmother too - after all she had been cared for by her for her first five years.

Play

Here we are talking about the kind of playing children do naturally, rather than 'play therapy' which needs the adult to have professional training.

There is little about play for the bereaved child which does not apply to every other child, except that there are increased opportunities to extend information: 'Your mummy bought this teddy for you'; 'She didn't like tomatoes either'.

However, knowing a little about some of the features of play which have been observed by experts may help carers to understand the bereaved young child a little better.

Examples:

If you invite your child to place toy people, animals, houses and plants in a sand tray, you will see whether all the people in his/her life are placed, and where, in relation to each other. You can prompt a little by saying 'Are you going to put --- in?', 'Is anybody missed out?' It is best not to make 'interpretations', just watch what he/she does spontaneously. From this you gain a picture of the child's world from *his/he*r perspective, not an adult's. Just doing this is therapeutic, and you could repeat the exercise in a year's time, or less, to see if it has changed.

At a slightly older age than two years, using drawing takes the static picture a little further: ask the child to draw a picture of everyone in the family, including him/herself, *doing something* – the rationale being that the addition of movement shows how the child sees himself/herself, also the dynamics of his/her family relationships.

A little more complex is a view by some experts that violent colours (red, purple, or black) often appear in drawings of troubled or frightened children (Santos 1991, Kübler-Ross 1981). It may be best to note the use of colour, but not use it as an indicator of feelings on its own.

Deciding on the need for professional help

This could come at any stage in childhood or adulthood when grief seems to be unresolved, as demonstrated by extreme disruption to normal life which has no apparent cause. In Em's case her extreme constipation landed her in hospital. The mention of a 'child psychologist' by the GP at the time, provoked a horrified response in Em's aunt - such was the taboo about mental illness - but he was possibly ahead of most in his thinking.

Depression is one of the consequences of unresolved grief for many people, both children and adult. Although a term used widely in Western society to cover all kinds of unhappiness, in this book it means very specifically a disabling form of emotional problem, and not as a mood which most of us experience during the ups, or rather downs, of everyday life. In the words of Rowe (1994, p. 1):

...there is a great difference between being depressed and being unhappy. When we are unhappy no matter what terrible things have happened to us, we still feel in contact with the world ..... when other people offer comfort and love we can feel it and it warms and supports us ..... when we are depressed we feel cut off from the world .....we are neither warmed nor supported by others..... we hurt ourselves and make life even more difficult.

The unreachable person is possibly the one whose grief is so profound and hidden that professional help is needed. Researchers at the University of Pittsburgh School of Medicine (2011) have found that 40 percent of children bereaved by sudden parental death will require intervention to prevent prolonged grief reaction and possible depression in adulthood. Relevantly for Em and many like her, these experts say that grief reactions in the surviving parent also need attention if, like her father, they appear to be extreme and prolonged, as their effects are possibly as detrimental to the child as the original loss.

Final thought: seeking therapy is not a sign of mental illness - it is a pointer to comparative mental health.

Conclusion

No one can be quite sure why some children survive trauma without damage, whilst others do not. However it appears that most need special help and some need *specialist* help.

This book advocates 'normal therapy': simply adding a little specialist knowledge to the intuitive skills which most carers already possess.

The therapy offered to Em succeeded through the quality and intensity of the relationship. This is the clue to working with bereaved children who appear to be rejecting their carers' efforts to be close to them.

What is equally crucial is the support which carers receive themselves when helping a child.

Finally, understanding some of the reactions to infant bereavement is a preparation for the inevitable death of parents at the more usual age.

Maggie Kindred

References

Baker, A. (2003) 'Family secrecy: a comparative study of juvenile sex offenders and youth with conduct disorders - Family and Couple Research'. *Family Process*, Spring, 2003.

Bayliss M. (1998) 'Counselling troubled children who have been abused'. In Z. Bear (ed) *Good practice in counselling children who have been abused*. London: Jessica Kingsley.

Bear, Z. (1998) *Good practice in counselling people who have been abused*. London, Jessica Kingsley.

Bettelheim, B (1950) *Love is not enough: the treatment of emotionally disturbed children*. New York: Free Press.

Bowlby, J. (1958) 'The Nature of the Childs Tie to His Mother'. *International Journal of Psychoanalysis*, 39, 350-371.

Bowlby, J. (1973) *Attachment and loss: Volume 2*. New York: Basic Books.

Bowlby, J. (1980) *Attachment and loss: Volume 3*. New York: Basic Books.

Carroll, D. (2008) *Psychology of language*. .Belmont CA:Thompson Higher Education.

Edelman, H. (1994) *Motherless Daughters: The Legacy of Loss*. Reading, MA:Addison-Wesley: Field, T. M. (ed.) (1995) *Touch in early development*. Hillsdale, NJ: Lawrence Erlbaum.

Hunter, M., & Struve, J. (1998) *The ethical use of touch in psychotherapy*. London: Sage.

Knable, J. (1981) 'Handholding: one means of transcending barriers of communication'. *Heart and Lung*, 1981, 10,6,1106.

Kübler-Ross, E. (ed) (1981) *Living with Death and Dying*. London: Souvenir Press.

Melhem, N., Porta, G., Shamseddeen, W., Walker Payne, M., Brent, D.(2011) 'Grief in Children and Adolescents Bereaved by Sudden Parental Death'. *Archives General Psychiatry* 2011, 68,911-919.

Mongillo, E., Briggs-Gowan, M., Ford, J., Carter, A (2009). 'Impact of Traumatic Life Events in a Community Sample of Toddlers'. *Journal of Abnormal Child Psychology*, 37, 455-468.

Montagu, A. (1986). *Touching; The Human Significance of the Skin*. New York: Harper and Row.

Rice, K., Groves, B. (2005). *Hope and healing: A caregiver's guide to helping young children affected by trauma*. Washington, DC: Zero to Three Press.

Rowe, D. (2003) *Depression: The Way Out of Your Prison*. Abingdon: Routledge.

Rutter, M., Taylor, E. (2002) *Child and adolescent psychiatry*. Chichester: Wiley-Blackwell.

Santos, C (1991) *Interpreting your Child's Drawings and Handwriting*. London: Robson Books.

Schore A., McIntosh J. (2011) 'Family law and the neuroscience of attachment, part I'.

Family Court Review 2011, 49.

Lightning Source UK Ltd.
Milton Keynes UK
UKOW040444081212

203338UK00001B/10/P